LET'S LOOK FOR
GARDEN BIRDS

HOW TO USE THIS BOOK

Gardens are wonderful places for birds to make their homes in and find food. Some birds are easy to see and hear, but others can be very shy and quiet. Use this guide to...

twiddle-oo, twiddle-eedee

...read all about these incredible creatures and find out what is so amazing about them.

blackcap

...see which garden birds you can find and identify. Then tick off the ones you spot.

...have fun playing with the bird stickers on the fold-out garden play scene at the back.

Looking at birds

Birds are feathery creatures that lay eggs. All birds
have beaks and wings, but not all of them can fly.
Get to know each bird's size, colour and beak shape.

PARTS OF A BIRD

Feathers
Birds are covered in
feathers – small ones
to keep them warm
and larger ones
to help them fly.

Eye

Beak
The shape of
a bird's beak
depends upon
what it eats.

Breast

Wing

Belly

Tail

Toe and claw
Birds, like this robin,
have four toes with
sharp claws for
gripping.

Amazing garden bird facts

Why do birds sing? Where do swallows and house martins go in winter? Find the answers below.

The first birds to sing in the morning are robins, wrens and blackbirds.

Birds have babies by laying eggs. They wouldn't be able to fly if they carried them in their tummies.

House martins and swallows fly all the way to Africa for the winter. They make their way back to the same nests the following summer.

Starlings gather in large numbers, especially in the autumn. In cities, you may get up to a million birds flying together.

A male bird may sing to attract a mate or to warn other male birds to stay away from his territory.

Even though robins can live to be over the age of 15, only one in four robins reaches the age of one.

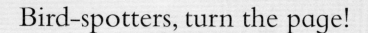

Bird-spotters, turn the page!

long-tailed tit

Easy-to-spot garden birds

You can see these birds all year round,
except for the swallow who flies to
Africa when it gets cold.

great tit ○

woodpigeon ○

chaffinch ○

blackbird ○

magpie ○

starling ○

wren ○

robin ◯

dunnock ◯

song thrush ◯

blue tit ◯

swallow ◯

sparrow ◯

jay ◯

Tick the birds off as you find them.

Harder-to-spot garden birds

coal tit ○

long-tailed tit ○

pied wagtail ○

○ jackdaw

nuthatch ○

mistle thrush ○

great spotted woodpecker ○

redwing ○

goldfinch ○

blackcap ○

○ collared dove

grey heron ○

○ green woodpecker

waxwing ○

means these birds are winter visitors.

What do they eat?

Not all birds eat the same things.
Look at the shape of their beaks. These tell
you a lot about the different types of food they eat.

Worms and snails
Birds, like blackbirds, have thin, pointy beaks – good for pulling up worms.

Fruit and berries
Most beaks are useful for picking fruits and berries.

Seeds and nuts
Short, sharp beaks are perfect for pecking at seeds and nuts.

Insects
Tasty grubs like this make a juicy meal for many birds. Almost any beak will do.

Fish
Herons use their long beaks to catch fish from garden ponds.